DISCARDED
MEMPHIS / SHELBY
COUNTY PUBLIC LIBRARY

ATTENTION DEFICIT HYPERACTIVITY DISORDER

Facts Parents Should Know

Nil A. Moore, Ed.D.

Introduction by Masoud S. Hejazi, M.D.

Illustrated by Dell Riggins

Counseling Center of Greensboro provides psychological and psychiatric evaluations and treatment for children, adolescents, and adults with Attention Deficit Hyperactivity Disorder, Learning Disabilities, Anxiety and Mood Disorders, Conduct Disorders, and Adjustment difficulties.

For more information, or to order a copy of this handbook, write or call:

> **Counseling Center of Greensboro**
> **101 S. Elm Street, Suite 325**
> **Greensboro, North Carolina 27401**
> **Phone: (336) 274-2100**
> **Fax: (336) 274-6366**
> **email: counselingcenterl@mybluelight.com**

Copyright © 2003 by Nil A. Moore, Ed.D.
Printed in U.S.A.
ISBN 0-9725765-0-9

All rights reserved. Unauthorized reproduction, in any manner, is prohibited.

Table of Contents

Introduction	1
Definition and Causes of ADHD	3
Types of ADHD	7
ADHD and Related Disorders	9
Diagnostic Process	13
Clinical Cases	21
Educational and Related Services	31
Treatment for ADHD	33
Strategies in dealing with ADHD children	37
Conclusion	41
References	43

Introduction
By Masoud S. Hejazi, M.D.

Attention Deficit Hyperactivity Disorder is the most common juvenile psychiatric disorder presenting to mental health workers including child psychiatrists and pediatricians. It is one of the major clinical and public health problems because of its associated morbidity and disability in children, adolescents and adults. Its relevance to society is significant in terms of financial costs, stress to families and impact on academic and vocational activities as well as having negative effects on self-esteem. Furthermore, the follow-up studies indicate that children with ADHD are at high risk for developing other psychiatric disorders and difficulties during childhood, adolescence and adulthood including antisocial behavior, substance abuse, and mood and anxiety disorders.

Dr. Moore, in her handout presented to parents and has discussed thoroughly and concisely the diagnostic criteria and also the prevalence and incidence rates of ADHD among children and adolescents. Different types of ADHDs have been brought to the reader's attention. ADHD has a high potential and tendency to be accompanied at times by other psychiatric disorders such as mood disorders including bipolar disorder, depressive disorder and anxiety disorders as well as substance abuse and learning disabilities. Conduct disorder and antisocial personality disorders are also seen more often with ADHD subtypes as well.

Dr. Moore has discussed concisely the diagnostic criteria and the appropriate treatments for this disorder including pharmacological approaches as well as cognitive and behavioral treatments. The pharmacological approach includes the usage of psychostimulants such as Ritalin, Dexedrine, amphetamines and derivatives, as well as usage of tricyclic antidepressants and non-tricyclic antidepressants such as bupropion and selective serotonin uptake inhibitors (i.e., Fluoxetine, Paroxetine, Sertraline, Fluvoxamine and Citalopram, Effexor, and alpha-2 agonists such as Clonidine and Guanfacine). Also, antipsychotic agents, particularly atypical antipscyhotics, such as Risperdal, Zyprexa and Seroquel have been used for not only the treatment of ADHD symptoms but also for other presenting psychiatric disorders in addition to ADHD. Atomoxetine, an investigational non-stimulant drug, is a selective norepinephrine reuptake inhibitor and has been shown to alleviate symptoms of ADHD. Once-daily Atomoxetine, which will be in the market sometime in 2003, has been reported to be effective through the evening and into the next morning providing continuous relief.

In this concise handout, emphasis has also been made regarding cognitive and behavior therapy with children and adolescents who suffer from ADHD as well as remedial school and academic work, particularly with children and adolescents who suffer from learning disabilities. Reading these facts, parents of ADHD children should gain thorough understanding of ADHD. This handbook is strongly recommended to those who have children or loved ones who are suspected of suffering from this disorder. The information provided by Dr. Moore in this brief handbook is based on the latest research data and treatment modalities for ADHD, and contains information that parents should know and communicate with healthcare providers treating their loved ones.

Definitions & Causes of ADHD

Attention Deficit Hyperactivity Disorder (ADHD) affects an estimated 5% to 10% of children and continues into adulthood in up to 50% to 60% of the cases. Accurate diagnosis is often difficult due to incomplete or brief assessments as well as the comorbidities that exist along with ADHD. Additionally, different psychological and psychiatric disorders can have similar symptoms as ADHD and the likelihood of another disorder has to be ruled out. Current research indicates that between 20% and 30% of children with ADHD have a parent or sibling who also has ADHD strongly suggesting that it is an inherited condition. According to Dr. Russell Barkley, an expert in the field, ADHD is a deficit related to the development and functioning of the prefrontal cortex of our brain. Dr. Herbert Quay's hypothesis on ADHD also supports Dr. Barkley's view of ADHD as being a developmental and neurological disorder. Researchers who investigated neuroanatomical regions of the brain, to identify problem areas, reported a strong possibility of two different locations involving the two types of ADHD. Based on this hypothesis, they suggest that ADHD with hyperactivity may be related to dopamine metabolism while the ADHD inattentive type may involve problems with metabolism of norepinephrine.

Although hereditary factors play a major role in the incidence of ADHD, the condition can be aggravated by complications during pregnancy, birth-related problems, exposure to toxins or neurological disease. Other risk factors involve mother's smoking, use of alcohol or drugs, and poor maternal health during pregnancy.

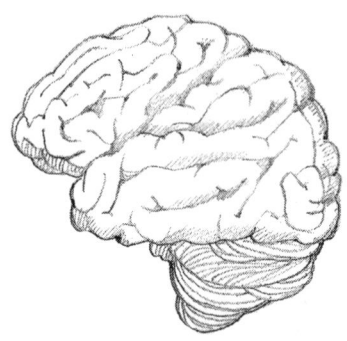

ADHD characteristics are similar throughout life span; however, they are displayed somewhat differently depending on the age of the individual. During preschool years, children with ADHD may be difficult to discipline and show more resistance to following rules set by their parents. They may also be overly active, refuse to take naps and may display impulsive behavior which can result in accidents and/or injuries. ADHD preschoolers are likely to be prone to more intense and frequent temper tantrums when they don't get their way. Ongoing problems with social interactions with other children and their parents, emotional difficulties which may consist of aggression or fearfulness are other characteristics that may be displayed during preschool years.

School-aged children with ADHD may display some of the above behaviors in school and may also be disruptive and easily distracted in the classroom. They often have difficulty completing assignments, forget to do homework, require assistance and reminding with daily chores, and exhibit oppositional behavior. Although temper tantrums may decrease with age the tendency for immediate gratification and lack of self-control often continue into adolescence and even into adulthood in cases where ADHD is severe.

Types of ADHD

Based on the Diagnostic and Statistical Manual of Mental Disorders, fourth edition (DSM-IV; American Psychiatric Association, 1994) ADHD has been classified into three subgroups as follows:
- **ADHD, Inattentive-Hyperactive-Impulsive Type**
- **ADHD, Predominately Inattentive Type**
- **ADHD, Predominately Hyperactive-Impulsive Type**

ADHD, Combined Types

These children will most often display characteristics such as being inattentive, overactive and impulsive. They often fail to complete requested tasks, display difficulties completing independent work and are described by their teachers as being disruptive in the classroom. Their inability to control their behavior sufficiently frequently results in adverse consequences. By talking excessively, interrupting others' conversations or blurting out comments often result in poor social and academic functioning. Furthermore, children with ADHD often seem to have difficulty learning from the mistakes they made in the past and have a poor sense of the future. Although they talk excessively their internal speech is frequently deficient and prevents them from reflecting on events before reacting, thereby contributing to poor decision-making and negative consequences. Drs. Barkley and Quay both emphasize that ADHD is a disorder involving problems with response inhibition. Delaying a response or an action enables the child to evaluate his decision to act. This ability to regulate one's own behavior involves the capacity to delay immediate rewards and pursue future goals. A child or an adolescent with ADHD is often impaired in doing what would be most favorable for his/her self-interest and future due to an inability to delay short-term reward.

ADHD, Predominantly Inattentive Type

The essential characteristics of children with this type of ADHD involve deficits in focused attention, being disorganized, slower perceptual-motor speed and sluggish processing of information. They may have problems with memory tasks, appear spacey and daydreamy, and display problems with reading comprehension often due to difficulties in tuning out distractions. Problems with completing homework and school assignments in a reasonable amount of time may also be observed by the child's parents and teachers. Such a child may continue to demonstrate poor study habits and his/her grades may become inconsistent often resulting in serious impairment in school functioning as academic demands increase.

ADHD and Related Disorders

Children with ADHD are at high risk of cognitive, developmental and academic difficulties, mood disorders, anxiety disorders, and conduct problems. These conditions are considered to be comorbid or coexisting features of ADHD.

It has been concluded that children with ADHD are more likely to have a learning disability (LD) in reading, math, spelling, or handwriting. Learning disability is defined as a significant discrepancy between the child's intellectual functioning and academic achievement and must be evaluated by standardized tests. It is estimated that about 25% of children with ADHD have at least one of LD in reading, spelling, math or handwriting.

In addition to being at higher risk for a learning disability, ADHD children tend to be deficient in their organizational skills and exhibit poor problem-solving strategies. They often leave assignments in school and lose important papers. Their approach to problem-solving is often impulsive and lacks foresight in terms of anticipating potential consequences for their actions. However, their difficulties are usually not due to lack of knowledge or skill but more the result of deficits in their executive processes believed to be mainly frontal and subcortical functions of the brain.

Most research studies investigating anxiety and mood disorders among children have suggested ADHD children having a higher incidence of depression and anxiety. On average, about 25%  of children with ADHD tend to have an anxiety disorder and up to 75% suffer from major depression or other mood disorders. Research also indicates that children who have one or both comorbid disorders tend to have low self-esteem and a negative outlook on the future compared to normal children. However, research investigations also suggest that ADHD children who may be anxious in childhood may experience symptoms of depression later in life as a consequence of having had to deal with the ADHD symptomatology over time. Given that ADHD children tend to lack appropriate social skills and have problems foreseeing social consequences they tend to be anxious in social settings. Children with ADHD, inattentive types are more likely to have social anxiety and may withdraw from activities that involve interaction with other children, thereby remain isolated. Likewise, children with hyperactivity may also have social anxiety; however, they are more likely to be aggressive rather than being withdrawn which often results in their being rejected by peers. About 6% of children with ADHD are likely to have a bipolar disorder (manic depression). ADHD children who also have bipolar disorder usually display more severe symptoms and often are diagnosed with conduct disorder.

ADHD children are inclined to report more somatic complaints in comparison to normal children. These complaints often consist of headaches and stomachaches and about physical problems such as allergies, colds, and ear infections. Research studies found about 25% to 35% ADHD adolescents as having somatization disorder.

Children with ADHD often experience problems getting to sleep and/or frequent awakening after falling asleep. Since most dreaming occurs during REM (rapid eye movement) sleep, an ADHD child who is deprived of it will tend to be more irritable, may overreact to external stimuli and experience attention and concentration problems. Approximately 50% - 60% of ADHD children are reported by their parents as waking up feeling tired in the morning.

Oppositional and defiant behavior and conduct problems are displayed more frequently and to a greater extent among ADHD children in comparison to normal children. Approximately 35% of

ADHD children are diagnosed with Oppositional Defiant Disorder and more than 25% meet the diagnostic criteria for Conduct Disorder. Oppositional behavior usually starts during preschool years and continue into adolescence. Temper tantrums, conflicts with parents regarding personal hygiene and resistance to parental discipline are common features during early years. In older children and adolescents the defiance is usually demonstrated by resisting to do household chores, being argumentative, disobedient, and skipping school. Conduct disordered children are usually physically aggressive and violate rules set by their parents and society. Furthermore, they display poor interpersonal skills and experience adjustment problems at school. Often, a child with a conduct disorder may end up being involved in drug use and delinquency during adolescence. Research also suggest impulsivity as being a major characteristic shared by both ADHD and conduct disorder. Consequently, an ADHD child or an adolescent with impulsivity is at higher risk for developing conduct disorder. It is also important to emphasize that conduct disorder coexisting with ADHD is one of the most difficult disorders to treat.

Diagnostic Process

Parents who suspect that their child may have ADHD should become familiar with its symptomatology in order to determine whether to seek professional assistance. Presently, the diagnostic criteria established in the fourth edition of the *Diagnostic and Statistical Manual of Mental Disorders (DSM-IV; American Psychiatric Association, 1994)* which has been developed from a committee of experts in the field is used to assist in the diagnosis of children with ADHD although it is not meant to be a diagnostic rule. This criteria can also be used to assist parents in determining whether their child exhibits some or all of these symptoms and need to be seen by a professional knowledgeable in diagnosing children with ADHD.

DSM-IV Criteria for ADHD

A. *Either 1 or 2:*

1. Six (or more) of the following symptoms of inattention have persisted for at least 6 months to a degree that is maladaptive and inconsistent with developmental level.

   Inattention
   - Often fails to give close attention to details or makes careless mistakes in school work, work or other activities.

- Often has difficulty sustaining attention in tasks or play activities.
- Often does not seem to listen when spoken to directly.
- Often does not follow through on instructions and fails to finish schoolwork, chores, or duties in the workplace (not due to oppositional behavior or failure to understand instructions).
- Often has difficulty organizing tasks and activities.
- Avoids, dislikes, or is reluctant to engage in tasks that require sustained mental effort (such as school work or homework).
- Often loses things necessary for tasks or activities (e.g., toys, school assignments, pencils, books, or tools).
- Is often easily distracted by extraneous stimuli.
- Often forgetful in daily activities.

2. Six (or more) of the following symptoms of hyperactivity, impulsivity have persisted for at least 6 months to a degree that is maladaptive and inconsistent with developmental level:

Hyperactivity
- Often fidgits with hands or feet or squirms in seat.
- Often leaves seat in classroom or in other situations in which remaining in seat is expected.
- Often runs about or climbs excessively in situations

in which it is inappropriate (in adolescents or adults, may be limited to subjective feelings of restlessness).
- Often has difficulty playing or engaging in leisure activities quietly.
- Is often "on the go" or often acts as if "driven by a motor".
- Often talks excessively.

Impulsivity
- Often blurts out answers before the questions have been completed.
- Often has difficulty awaiting turn.
- Often interrupts or intrudes on others (e.g. butts into conversations or games).

B. *Some hyperactive-impulsive or inattentive symptoms that caused impairment were present before age 7 years.*

C. *Some impairment from the symptoms is present in two or more settings (at school or work and at home).*

D. *There must be clear evidence of clinically significant impairment in social, academic, or occupational functioning.*

E. *The symptoms do not occur exclusively during the course of Pervasive Developmental Disorder, Schizophrenia or other Psychotic Disorder, and are not accounted for by another mental disorder (e.g., Mood Disorder, Anxiety Disorder, Dissociative Disorder or a Personality Disorder).*

After reviewing the DSM-IV criteria for ADHD, if parents recognize that their child has displayed hyperactivity, inattention and impulsivity in excess compared to other children his/her age for at least 6 months or longer they may consider seeking professional assistance. Children with ADHD, combined types, have poor self-control and usually tend to be more active, inattentive, and impulsive. However, if the child's parents notice that the problems are more in the area of inattention, being disorganized and forgetful and do not involve hyperactivity or impulsivity, they may have a reason to suspect that their child may have predominantly inattentive type ADHD. At this point, the professional to contact may be a psychologist with expertise in ADHD, a child psychiatrist, the child's pediatrician or the family physician who can refer the child to an ADHD specialist for an evaluation. Prior to an ADHD evaluation it would be best for the child to have a physical examination performed by his physician to rule out the possibility of any medical problems which may result in the symptoms.

As a first step, an ADHD specialist will obtain a thorough background information prior to scheduling a comprehensive psychological evaluation. Gathering of relevant background information is a crucial step in the diagnostic process. Background data consist of obtaining information regarding the maternal health during pregnancy, delivery procedure and infant health following birth and as an infant along with developmental history. Child's parents would also provide information as to the activity level of their child and academic history if the child is of school age. This information would also include the child's adaptive and social functioning and family history of ADHD and/or other related disorders. Any prior psychological and/or neurological evaluations that may have been done should be obtained prior to conducting in-depth assessment. Finally, child's school records consisting of behavioral and academic functioning would be requested from the school child attends with the written consent of the parents.

The next step would involve the evaluation of the child's intellectual functioning, visual-motor integration skills, academic achievement, attention/concentration, and emotional and behavioral functioning. The psychologist's observations during the evaluation process, in terms of the child's approach toward tasks, motivation and effort put forth during testing, activity level, attention/focusing, sustained concentration and his/her ability to follow instruction will also provide highly valuable information in making an accurate diagnosis.

Following the evaluation process the ADHD specialist will meet with the child's parents to go over the findings of the assessment and the diagnosis. There will be a typed report containing the evaluation findings which the specialist will explain to the parents in detail to ensure that they have full understanding of the diagnosis of ADHD and how it was arrived at. The parents will be encouraged to ask questions pertaining to the diagnosis of ADHD and any comorbid condition that may exist. The specialist will make recommendations which may involve medical and behavioral treatments. The child's parents will also be provided with information regarding the type of accommodations and assistance the child's school can provide under Public Law 94-142 involving the Education for All Handicapped Childrens Act which later was amended by Public Law 101-476, the Individuals with Disabilities Education Act (IDEA).

Impact of the ADHD Diagnosis

Most parents who are told that their child has ADHD may accept the diagnosis and even feel relief. After all, parents who bring their child to an ADHD specialist for an evaluation have been dealing with the ADHD symptomatology of their child for quite some time without the certainty that their child has ADHD. In fact, they may have felt that their parenting skills were inadequate and possibly contributing to their child's problems. Along with acceptance comes the acknowledgment that they will need to acquire special skills and learn new strategies in helping their child deal more effectively with ADHD.

Parents who did not suspect anything was wrong with their child may engage in denial of the ADHD diagnosis. Usually such a parent may have taken the child to a specialist because the child's teacher may have suggested the evaluation as a result of the observations of the child's problem behaviors. When parents find themselves opposing a diagnosis the best course would be to seek a second opinion from another professional who knows about ADHD.

Most parents may also experience grief-like reaction to their child's ADHD when informed that their child has a neurological disorder. Some parents may be concerned about their ability to manage their child's special needs and others may be concerned about their child's future and whether ADHD will limit his/her success academically and otherwise. For most parents this is a temporary state and eventually they adapt to the existence of ADHD and get involved in the daily responsibilities of taking care of their child's needs. If the grieving continues then it would be wise to consider short-term counseling with a mental health professional who is experienced in doing therapy with parents of ADHD children.

Clinical Cases

In order to better demonstrate the evaluation process involved in the assessment of ADHD children two actual cases are presented. The names of the children have been changed to protect their identities.

JASON

Background Information

Jason was referred for a psychological evaluation by his parents to determine if he had ADHD and/or a learning disability. His parents reported problems with attention/concentration, impulsivity, low frustration tolerance, and difficulties with controlling his temper. He was reported as being noncompliant and argumentative especially when he didn't get his way. Jason also reported that he felt depressed and subdued most of the time and did not feel happy. He also did not have many friends. He reported having difficulty falling asleep at night. Jason was an 8 year old boy who was in the third grade and lived with his parents and a younger brother. His mother reported that her pregnancy was full term and delivery was normal. Jason accomplished his developmental milestones accordingly. He had been diagnosed as having ADHD by his pediatrician about a year ago and had been taking Adderall and Ritalin. According to Jason's father the psychostimulants Jason was on had helped him tremendously with his attention span and school work. However, he continued to have anger and agitation and seemed unhappy.

After the initial interview and collection of background information, Jason's parents were given the Conners' Parent Rating scales to evaluate his behavior in the home. Conners' Teacher Rating Scale was sent to Jason's third grade teacher to assess classroom behavior. Jason was scheduled for a psychological evaluation.

Behavioral Observations

Jason was serious and anxious during the initial stages of the evaluation. He had taken the morning dose of Ritalin on the first day of the evaluation. He seemed motivated and worked consistently. However, he was easily frustrated when he was not successful on a task. On the second day of the evaluation, with the suggestion of the clinician, Jason had not taken his medicine. Although he was not fidgety nor hyper, his attention/focusing varied and he left several math problems undone until he was reminded to go back and complete them.

Evaluation Procedures

Jason was administered the Wechsler Intelligence Scale for Children, Third. Ed. (WISC-III), Bender Visual Motor Gestalt Test, Woodcock-Johnson Tests of Achievement-Revised, House-Tree-Person Test, and Piers-Harris Children's Self-Concept Scale. The above tests would assess Jason's intellectual functioning, visual-motor integration, academic achievement and his emotional condition.

Evaluation Results

Jason was found to be functioning in the average range in intellectual ability. His WISC-III Full scale IQ was in the 42nd percentile. His visual-motor integration skills were also in the average range consistent with his cognitive functioning. However, his organization and planning abilities, on the Bender, were poor. Jason's academic skills in reading and math were at beginning-second grade level with written expression being at third grade level. There was a significant discrepancy between his intellectual functioning and his math performance, suggesting the possibility of a learning disability in that area.

Jason's parents' ratings on the Conners' Scales indicated significant problems in areas involving restless-disorganized behavior, compulsive tendencies, some hyperactivity and conduct problems.

ADHD Rating Scales completed, separately, by Jason's parents demonstrated problems with attention/focusing, impulsivity, and hyperactivity.

Conners' Teacher Rating Scale completed by Jason's teacher indicated significant problems in areas involving emotional indulgence (e.g., temper outbursts, mood changes, being easily frustrated) and moderate conduct problems (e.g., stubborn, disrupts other children).

Jason's performance on tests assessing his emotional condition (House-Tree-Person Test and Piers Harris Scale) suggested low self-esteem coupled with inferiority feelings and perfectionistic tendencies. He seemed to be mildly depressed and anxious and had a tendency to display poor impulse control when frustrated. Jason also had difficulties in interpersonal relations with his parents, peers and his brother.

Conclusion and Recommendation

The finding of the evaluation suggested the existence of ADHD, inattentive and impulsive type symptomatology consisting of attention/focusing problems, distractibility, excessive talking in class, being disorganized, perfectionistic tendencies, impulsivity, and significant problems with emotional control. It was concluded that Jason's symptomatology would significantly impair his academic progress. The results of the evaluation were shared with Jason's parents and they were recommended to schedule an appointment with the Counseling Center psychiatrist for medication reevaluation to determine the best medication regimen for Jason. Additional suggestions offered were as follows:

1. It is recommended that the IEP team at Jason's school review the findings of the evaluation along with his classroom performance to determine the best educational program for him. He appears to be eligible for "Other Health Impaired" program due to his ADHD. He also meets the LD criteria in math and is likely to need academic assistance in that area.

2. In the home, a consistent schedule should be set for doing homework, chores, playtime, eating and sleeping.

3. Family therapy is recommended to assist Jason's parents in establishing and implementing a behavior plan to help Jason develop more self-control, reduce feelings of frustration, and improve his relationship with his parents and his brother.

Treatment Outcome

Jason is presently 15 years old and attends ninth grade. He is currently on Adderall XR and Effexor XR. His medication regimen is presently being monitored by the Center psychiatrist. Earlier he had been on Adderall and Paxil and did fairly well on this regimen for quite some time until about six months ago when Paxil did not seem to be as effective for his depressive symptoms. During the last 6 years, Jason and his parents have kept in touch with this clinician and worked on different issues during family sessions. Jason also attended group sessions, soon after the evaluation was completed. The group consisted of 4 - 6 children diagnosed with ADHD and met once a month at this clinician's office. The goal of the group meetings was to facilitate appropriate social interaction and improve interpersonal skills.

Jason and his parents continue to attend family sessions every 6 - 8 weeks. Jason has been doing well in school and has learned to control his temper more effectively. He also has some friends and gets along better with his parents and his brother. Jason's parents seem to be quite satisfied with his progress.

SANDY

Background Information

Sandy was referred for a psychological evaluation due to difficulties with attention/concentration, following instructions and establishing appropriate relationships with peers. Her mother reported that Sandy tended to be oppositional and argumentative in the home and at times she was aggressive with other children. She was also reported as having difficulties going to bed at night. Sandy was an 8 year old girl who was in the second grade and lived with her adoptive parents. Both parents were employed. Sandy's mother reported that Sandy had an extensive vocabulary and was highly verbal when she was adopted at age three. However, she wasn't toilet trained until she was 4 years old and she still wet the bed when she was six years old. When she was younger she exhibited fear of her parents' dying and had nightmares. She had been screened for ADHD at her school the previous year and the results indicated average range intellectual ability and existence of overactive and distractible behavior in the classroom. She was also reported as having social problems.

Following the initial interview and collection of background data, Sandy's parents were given the Conners' Parent Rating Scales to complete and her teacher was also requested to complete the Conners' Teacher Rating Scale in order to evaluate Sandy's behavior in the home and at school. Additionally, she was scheduled for an evaluation.

Behavioral Observations

Sandy was very friendly and talkative during the evaluation sessions. She indicated that she was not good in drawing when she was shown the geometric shapes (Bender Gestalt Test) she had to copy. She also didn't like the math tests and indicated that she was getting bored and wanted to quit. She tended to give detailed answers in responding to test questions and seemed to brag about how much she knew ("I know everything"). She often tried to give up on tasks that required sustained concentration. Her behavior during testing sessions was disinhibited, restless, and anxious at times.

Evaluation Procedures

Sandy was administered the Wechsler Intelligence Scale for Children, Third Ed. (WISC-III), Bender Visual Motor Gestalt Test, Woodcock-Johnson III Tests of Achievement, Sentence Completion Test, and House-Tree-Person Test. The above tests would assess her intellectual functioning, visual-motor integration, academic achievement and her emotional condition.

Evaluation Results

Sandy was found to be functioning in the high average range in intellectual ability. Her WISC-III Full Scale IQ was in the 77th percentile. Her WISC-III profile indicated high average verbal abilities and average visual spatial skills. Her strengths were in areas involving word knowledge, logical thinking and grouping ability and verbal memory. Her weaknesses involved visual attention to detail, part-whole conceptualization of visual stimuli and social judgement/common sense. Although Sandy's reading skills were at mid-third grade level, her reading comprehension was at end-second grade level. Her math skills were also at second grade level. Sandy performed at first grade level on timed tests involving reading and math suggesting attention/concentration weaknesses which may have slowed her speed of performance.

Sandy's parents' ratings on the Conners' Scales indicated significant problems in Oppositional, Cognitive Problems/Innattention, Hyperactivity, Social Problems, Conners' ADHD Index, Conners' Global Index: Restless-Impulsive, Conners' Global Index: Total, DSM-IV: Inattentive, DSM-IV: Hyperactive-Impulsive, DSM-IV: Total domains. Her teacher's ratings on the Conners' Scale assessing Sandy's classroom behavior also showed significant problems in similar areas.

Sandy's performance on the projective measures (Sentence Completion and House-Tree-Person Tests) revealed low self-esteem and feelings of insecurity. She appeared to have difficulties with self-control and tended to be disinhibited. She also had a tendency to get angry when external limitations were placed upon her behavior. Finally, there were indications of anxiety mixed with depressive tendencies and fear of the future.

Conclusions and Recommendations

The results of this evaluation suggested the existence of ADHD, inattentive and impulsive type symptomatology consisting of poor attention/focusing, difficulties with sustained concentration, restlessness, excessive talking, distractibility and difficulties with managing behavior. It was concluded that Sandy's ADHD symptomatology would significantly impair her academic progress. The findings of the evaluation were shared with Sandy's parents and they were recommended to schedule an appointment with the Counseling Center psychiatrist for medication consultation to determine if she would benefit from being on a pyschostimulant. Additional suggestions offered were as follows:

1. It is recommended that the IEP team at Sandy's school review the findings of the evaluation along with her classroom performance to determine the best educational program for her. She appears to be eligible for "Other Health Impaired" program due to her ADHD.

2. Sandy would perform best in a structured setting where consequences for breaking rules and rewards for desirable behavior are clearly defined and followed through by the parents and classroom teacher.

3. In the home, there should be a consistent schedule set for doing homework, playtime, eating, and sleeping.

4. All school and homework requirements should be broken into small segments with short breaks in between to help maintain Sandy's interest on tasks and also reduce frustration.

5. Extended time on all timed tasks and tests should be allowed at school if Sandy needs it.

6. Sandy may need to have academic assistance in math as she is reported to have difficulties in the classroom.

7. Individual and family counseling will be offered to help Sandy cope more effectively with ADHD characteristics, improve self-control and self-esteem and reduce anxiety.

Treatment Outcome

Sandy is presently on Concerta for her ADHD symptomatology and also on Paxil for her anxiety mixed with depressive symptoms. She has been attending individual therapy sessions on a regular basis with the clinician. Both parents are very involved in her treatment and they also meet with the clinician periodically to report on her progress. As of this date, Sandy is in the third grade and receives some special education services in math at her school. She has shown progress academically and behaviorally and her parents are satisfied with the treatment outcome.

Educational & Related Services

Many students with ADHD qualify for special education services under the Section 504 of the Rehabilitation Act of 1973 (Public Law 93-112) since Individuals with Disabilities Education Act (IDEA; 1991, Public Law 101-476) recognized that ADHD can be a disabling condition. This law provides a free appropriate education such as special education and related services to children with ADHD free of cost to parents. The services provided and accommodations made must be included in an individualized education program (IEP) for children who have been diagnosed with ADHD. An IEP is a written contract that documents types of special education and related services that will be provided and how progress toward the goals stated will be measured. In order to qualify for services based on the IDEA a student would have to be diagnosed with one or more of the disabilities stated in this law following a psychological evaluation validating the need for special education services. Children diagnosed with ADHD usually are eligible to receive services under the "Other Health Impaired" category. This category includes chronic and acute impairments which contribute to limited alertness. ADHD student's attention and focusing difficulties in the classroom most often will result in impairment of academic functioning, thereby making the student eligible for special education services.

ADHD diagnosis by a physician or psychiatrist is not adequate to provide special education services to a student. Based on the IDEA, an individualized evaluation must be conducted by a multidisciplinary team such as a psychologist, medical doctor, and at least one teacher who has knowledge of the child's disability. Additionally, a school district is responsible to evaluate the eligibility of a student who is referred for an evaluation by his/her parents. Parents also have a right to request a due process hearing if their child is denied an evaluation or if the school district decides not to provide special education services after the evaluation is conducted.

School interventions can have a strong influence on ADHD children since the ADHD symptomatology and the coexisting conditions are highly responsive to external variables. ADHD students require more structured environments, consistently implemented positive and negative consequences, and assistance and/or accommodations with their schoolwork. To maximize an ADHD student's academic success it is crucial that there is a collaboration between home and school.

Treatment for ADHD

Most authorities in the field recommend a combination of cognitive and behavioral therapy and family interventions along with the use of psychostimulant for effective management of ADHD. Stimulant medication treatment is highly effective for controlling attention problems and decreasing hyperactivity and physical restlessness in ADHD children. Research indicates that child's compliance with parent and teacher also increases with the use of a psychostimulant. However, medication does not compensate for daily functioning difficulties, especially if the child has a coexisting disorder that needs to be addressed. Most children with ADHD will require individual and family therapy and other strategies as part of their longterm treatment.

Medical Treatment

Although psychostimulants such as Ritalin, Concerta, Adderall and Dexedrine are most effective in treating ADHD in children and adolescents 20% of children may not show a positive response to the medication and a small percentage of children may display side effects which may result in discontinuation of the medication. In such cases medications other than psychostimulants may be considered since some efficacy of these drugs have been shown in the treatment of ADHD symptomatology. These medications consist mainly of

antidepressants and anticonvulsants which are helpful for some ADHD children who have not shown any benefit from being on psychostimulants or may have experienced side effects. Another factor for the use of other than psychostimulant medications would be in cases when the child has a comorbid condition along with ADHD. Clonidine has shown to be effective for some ADHD children. It is usually prescribed in combination with a psychostimulant mainly with children who have ADHD and also may be oppositional or defiant. In other cases Clonidine may be used with an ADHD child who experiences significant problems calming down and going to sleep at night. Tenex is another medication prescribed for ADHD children who tend to be easily agitated and/or aggressive. These medications modify behavior by changing the brain chemistry. Evidence strongly suggests that these drugs as well as the psychostimulants increase the norepinephrine and dopamine levels in the frontal part of the brain. The most common side effect of stimulant medications involve mild loss of appetite in some children which has been found to be usually short-term. Most family physicians, pediatricians and child psychiatrists recommend drug holidays during school breaks and over the summer. In severe cases of ADHD stimulants are also used effectively with younger children under 5 years of age especially when behavioral interventions fail to be effective.

Behavioral Treatment

A combination of behavioral and cognitive therapy approaches are often used with ADHD children who display aggressive and impulsive behavior. By teaching anger management strategies and social skills training children with ADHD can reduce their impulsive and aggressive behavior and improve peer relations. Cognitive therapy strategies often focus on improving the child's self-control skills by teaching the child to "stop and think" in order to reduce impulsive actions, and improve decision-making and problem-solving skills. ADHD children usually begin to have social problems in preschool years. Their hyperactivity, impulsivity and distractibility often prevent them from learning the basic social rules. The deficiency in their social skills continue into later years and often results in social isolation and a poor self-image. Individual therapy with an ADHD child can focus on helping the child develop more effective coping skills in dealing with ADHD characteristics, improve social skills, and self-esteem.

Parents can be taught to be more helpful in assisting their child's monitoring of his/her behavior by becoming therapeutic agents themselves in the treatment process. However, if one or both parents appear to display ADHD characteristics and/or have psychological or psychiatric problems, they would be recommended to have a psychological evaluation and seek individual therapy in order to be able to help manage their child more effectively.

Family Intervention

Parents of ADHD children tend to be under a great deal of distress and thereby often become negative in their interactions with their child. Most of them realize their inability to deal with their child's problems and may begin to feel inadequate about their parenting skills. Parent training involves teaching parents of ADHD children more effective ways to manage their child's behavior. As they experience improvement in their ability to handle their child's behavior, they are likely to feel more competent and experience less distress and frustration.

Strategies in Dealing With ADHD Children

1. As a parent, effective management of an ADHD child requires understanding about ADHD which consist of being educated about the characteristics of ADHD and multiple problems ADHD children experience daily in their lives.

2. Children with ADHD experience less stress when their daily routine is consistent with specified periods set for bedtime, chores, doing homework, playtime, dinner and so on.

3. Parents need to set the ground rules their ADHD child has to follow and specify consequences for breaking rules and rewards for desirable behavior. It is best to write these rules clearly and place them in a visible location in the home. Consistently sticking to the written rules will be necessary in order to help an ADHD child develop good habits.

4. When giving instructions or directions to an ADHD child, parents should make certain that they are simple and clearly stated and should not exceed one or two instructions at a time.

5. The child should have a quiet location, away from distractions, where he/she can do school related tasks.

6. Parents should try to be positive in communicating to their child what they would like him/her to do. It is more effective to tell a child the desirable behavior you would like him/her to engage in rather than telling what you would like your child not to do.

7. Although an ADHD child's behavior can often be irritating and annoying, parents should refrain from becoming angry. An angry parent loses effectiveness in getting their child to comply and do what is appropriate.

8. Repeating requests and directions are ineffective ways to discipline ADHD children. Instead, it is best to tell the child what you need to say once and in a positive manner, briefly and firmly.

9. ADHD children often have difficulty switching from an enjoyable activity to a boring activity. To reduce conflict in such situations

it is best to allow the child to engage in the fun activity only after the child has done the work expected, such as homework or chores.

10. Children with ADHD usually are interested in short-term goals and immediate gratification. Parents can redirect the child's behavior toward future goals in order to help their child develop self-control.

11. A written behavioral contract negotiated between parents and their ADHD child, or adolescent, can help the child develop better daily habits by providing incentives. The contract can specify each party's obligations and state what the consequences will be when the child performs his/her responsibilities such as cleaning room, making bed, doing homework and so on.

12. Caring for an ADHD child is a mentally and emotionally exhausting task. Consequently, regular time away from the child will be helpful for the wellbeing of the parents.

Conclusion

Existing research suggests that approximately 50% to 60% of ADHD children continue to display ADHD symptomatology into adulthood. ADHD can affect many areas of an individual's life. It may be noticed as the person having a low tolerance for frustration, emotional overreactivity, poor impulse control, occupational and marital difficulties, social problems, procrastination, difficulties with being organized and high rates of divorce. Furthermore, adults with ADHD often have coexisting disorders such as depression, anxiety, substance dependence or abuse. There are indications that ADHD children or adolescents with conduct and aggression problems are at greater risk of continuing to have these problems into adulthood. Research shows that participation by the ADHD children in a long-term treatment program, consisting of multiple interventions, result in enhanced self-esteem, less delinquency, and a better future as adults. ADHD is a lifelong malady and, if untreated, can result in confounding outcomes in an individual's life.

References

Abikoff, H. & Klein, R.G. (1992). Attention-deficit hyperactivity and conduct disorder: Comorbidity and implications for treatment. *Journal of Consulting and Clinical Psychology,* 60, 881-892.

American Psychiatric Association. (1994). *Diagnostic and statistical manual of mental disorders* (4th ed., DSM-IV.) Washington, DC: Author.

Barkley, R.A. (1995). *Taking charge of ADHD.* New York: Guilford Press.

Barkley, R.A. (1997). Behavioral inhibition, sustained attention and executive functions: Constructing a unifying theory of ADHD. *Psychological Bulletin,* 121:65-94.

Barkley, R.A. (1998). *Attention deficit hyperactivity disorder.* New York: Guilford Press.

Barkley, R.A. (2001). The executive funtions and self-regulation: An evolutionary neuropsychological perspective. *Neuropsychology Review,* 11: 1-29.

Barkley, R. A., DuPaul, G.J., & McMurray, M.B. (1990). A comprehensive evaluation of attention deficit disorder with and without hyperactivity. *Journal of Consulting and Clinical Psychology,* 58: 775-789.

Biderman, J., Newcom, J. & Sprich, S. (1991). Comorbidity of attention deficit hyperactivity disorder with conduct, depressive, anxiety, and other disorders. *American Journal of Psychiatry,* 148: 564-577.

Bukstein, O.G., & Kolko, D.J. (1998). Effects of Methylphenidate on aggressive urban children with attention deficit hyperactivity disorder. *Journal of Clinical Child Psychology,* 27: 340-351.

Chelune, G.J., Ferguson, W., Koon, R., & Dickey, T.O. (1986). Frontal Lobe Disinhibition in Attention Deficit Disorder. *Child psychiatry & human development,* 16: 221-234.

Cunningham, C.E., & Barkley, R.A. (1979). The interactions of hyperactive and normal children with their mothers during free play and structured tasks. *Child development,* 50: 217-224.

Diaz, R.M., & Berk, L.E. (1992). *Private speech: From social interaction to self-regulation.* Erlbaum, Mahwah: New Jersey.

Dykman, R.A., & Ackerman, P.T. (1993). Behavioral subtypes of attention deficit disorder. *Exceptional children,* 60:132-141.

Fisher, B.C. (1998). *Attention deficit disorder misdiagnosis.* Boca Raton: CRC Press.

Hallowell, E.M., & Ratey, J.J. (1994). *Driven to distraction.* New York: Pantheon Books.

Mezzacappa, E., Kindlon, D., & Earls, F. (1999). Relations of age to cognitive and motivational elements of impulse control in boys with and without externalizing behavior problems. *Journal of Abnormal Psychology,* 27: 473-483.

Mirsky, A.F. (1996). Disorders of attention: A neuropsychological perspective. In R.G. Lyon & N.A. Krasnegor (eds.), *Attention, memory, and executive function,* Paul H. Brookes, Baltimore, pp. 71-96.

Overmeyer, S., & Taylor, E. (1999). Annotation: Principles of treatment for hyperkinetic disorder: Practice approaches for the U.K. *Journal of Child Psychology and Psychiatry,* 40: 1147-1157.

Quay, H.C. (1997). Inhibition and Attention Deficit Hyperactivity Disorder. *Journal of Abnormal Child Psychology,* 25: 7-13.

Sudderth, D.B., & Kandel, J. (1997). *Adult ADD.* Rocklin, CA: Prima Publishing.

Weiss, G., & Hechtman, L.T. (1994). *Hyperactive children grown up (2nd Ed.),* New York: Guilford Press.

Wilens, T.E., Biederman, J., Mick, E., & Spencer, T.J. (1995). A systematic assessment of tricyclic antidepressants in the treatment of adult attention deficit hyperactivity disorder. *Journal of Nervous and Mental Disease,* 183: 48-50.

Woodrich, D. (1994). *Attention deficit hyperactivity disorder.* Baltimore: Paul H. Brookes Publishing Co.